949.6

WITHDRAWN

WOODLAWN MIDDLE SCHOOL
6362 RFD Gilmer RD.
Long Grove, IL 60047
(847) 949-8013

WOODLAWN MIDDLE SCHOOL
6362 RFD Gilmer RD.
Long Grove, IL 60047
(847) 949-8113

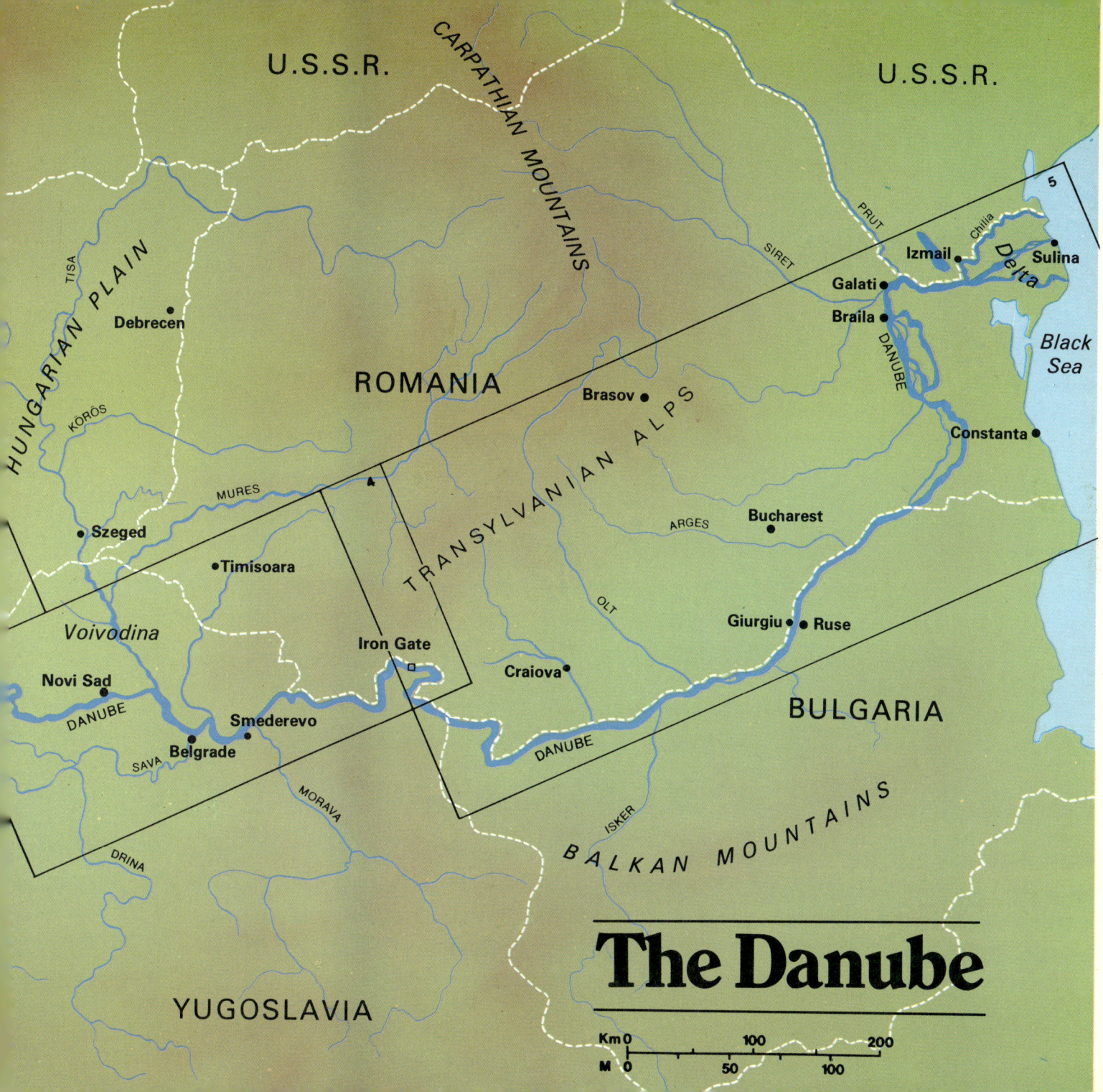

The Danube

A journey down the Danube from source to delta, from the Black Forest to the Black Sea, is a fascinating journey through European history.

Ancient settlements more than 8,000 years old have been discovered along the Danube banks. Part of the river was for centuries the boundary between the Roman Empire and the northern "barbarians". Attila the Hun, the Crusaders, and the Turks have all marched along its banks or sailed along its course. For the Gypsies, the Danube was "the dustless road".

In this book we travel from peaceful source to fantastic delta, examining the Danube as it was in history and as it is today.

Frontispiece   *The Hungarian parliament building overlooking the Danube – one of the most impressive sights of Budapest*

Rivers of the World

The Danube

C A R Hills

Wayland/Silver Burdett

Rivers of the World

The Amazon
The Danube
The Ganges
The Mississippi
The Nile
The Rhine

Copyright © 1979 Wayland Publishers Limited
First published in 1979 by
Wayland Publishers Limited
49 Lansdowne Place, Hove
East Sussex BN3 1HF, England
ISBN 0 85340 456 9

Published in the United States by
Silver Burdett Company, Morristown,
New Jersey.
1978 printing ISBN 0 382 06204 3

Phototypeset by Trident Graphics Limited, Reigate, Surrey
Printed in England by Loxley Brothers Limited

Contents

Introduction: the Dustless Road	9
Through Highland Germany	15
Into Austria	23
The Great Plains	33
To the Iron Gates	43
Towards the Delta	55
Facts and Figures	62
Glossary	63
Further Reading	64
Index	65

8 **Above** *This pool at Donaueschingen is the "official" source of the Danube which tourists visit. The real sources are several streams higher up in the hills*

Introduction: the Dustless Road

The Danube is a great river uniting many different landscapes and peoples. It is 2,850 km (1,770 miles) long, which makes it the longest river in Europe apart from the Volga. Its drainage basin covers an area more than nine times as large as England, Scotland and Wales put together. It has more than 300 tributary rivers, many of them important rivers in their own right. Eight countries are washed by its waters – West Germany, Austria, Czechoslovakia, Hungary, Yugoslavia, Romania, Bulgaria and the Soviet Union. All the water in Romania's numerous rivers flows into it as well as nearly all of Austria's water and almost two-thirds of Yugoslavia's.

Throughout history the river has been tremendously important to the development and settlement of Europe and as a highway for trade. However the amount of river traffic has perhaps been rather less than you might expect for such a long and powerful river. Here the Danube contrasts strongly with the Rhine, which is a much shorter river but indisputably one of the world's great highways. There are many reasons for this. Some of them are to do with the Danube itself, for it is a rather wild force of nature. The amount of water in the river can change very rapidly, owing to the many climatic regions that it and its tributaries pass through. Huge floods can result which, in the past, have done immense damage to Hungary and Yugoslavia. Sometimes, too, there can be very shallow sections in the course. In some places there are rocks or dangerous gorges; in others the river divides into many channels with islands in between. On an average of sixty-five days a year there may be ice. Navigation has never been easy on the Danube.

Some of the reasons for the comparative lack of traffic are also to do with human history. The Danube begins as a mountain stream in the highland country of West Germany and Austria. Then it flows for thousands of kilometres as a "flatland" river through the marshy plains of south-eastern Europe. This region has never been as highly developed as western Europe and trade and traffic have all too often been interrupted by wars and bloody invasions. The nineteenth century Austrian statesman, Metternich, once said: "Eastwards from Vienna, the Orient begins". It is certainly true that we often know too little about these regions. They seem even more remote to us in

Right *The Breg, a little stream which becomes part of the great Danube*

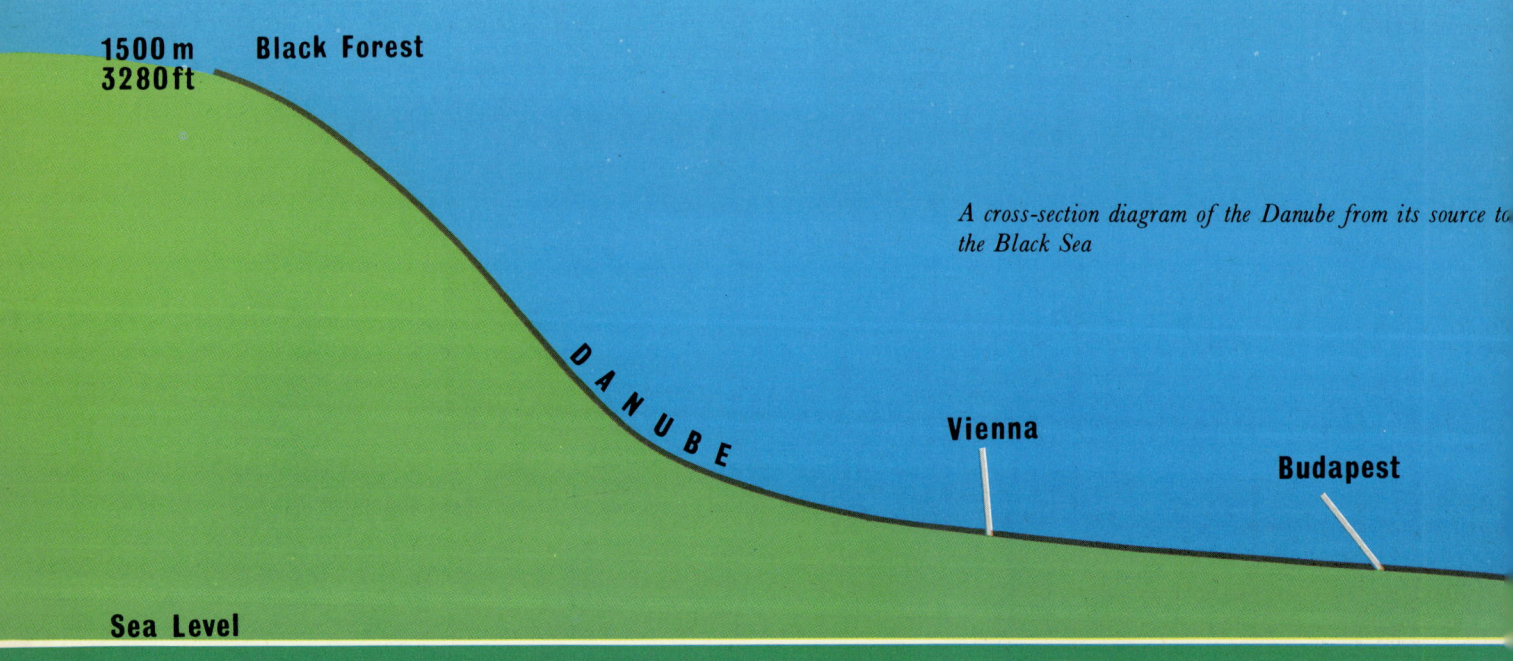

A cross-section diagram of the Danube from its source to the Black Sea

Belgrade   Iron Gates   Black Sea

2850 km   1770 miles

Above There are many fine towns, castles and churches along the Danube. This beautiful stained-glass window in Ulm cathedral shows the murder of Abel by his brother, Cain

modern times, because ever since the Second World War the countries through which the Danube flows after Vienna have been under Communist rule. In this book we shall learn more about these countries and their history.

But the Danube is too great a river for these problems to have prevented human development. For thousands of years traders, migrants, invaders, armies and voyagers have passed along its banks, built their settlements by its waters and used it to defend their land. The ancient Greeks, 2,700 years ago, were trading all along the lower course of the river. The Romans, who never subdued all of northern Europe, made the Danube an important northern frontier to their empire two thousand years ago and their patrol ships sailed along it. Vienna, Budapest and Belgrade, the present-day capitals of Austria, Hungary and Yugoslavia respectively, were all Roman settlements.

Later, the Danube became a frontier for the Byzantine and Turkish empires also. Today it helps to separate Hungary and Czechoslovakia, Yugoslavia and Romania, Bulgaria and Romania and Romania and the Soviet Union. This long history has left its banks studded with towns and castles.

In modern times river traffic has developed slowly but steadily; an international commission to improve navigation was set up as long ago as 1856. For some time now all eight countries along the river have been operating large fleets of trading boats. Passenger services, once extensive, are now generally only for holidaymakers. Perhaps the Gypsies, who followed the river in their long migration from India into Europe, summed up the Danube best – they called it "the dustless road".

How did this great river come into being? The Danube was formed at about the time, 30 million years ago, that the greatest mountains of Europe, the Alps, were built up in great folds of rock during a period of earth disturbances. Other mountains continued the Alps to the east – the Carpathians and Balkans. In the lowland trough to the north of the new mountains, the river began to form. What are now the plains of Hungary were at that time a vast lake, but this was drained by the earth movements and the river's course was virtually complete.

The Danube has had a long, sometimes troubled, history. It also has a bright future. The regions through which it flows, up until now often peasant countries, are developing fast and river traffic is greatly increasing. New projects are connecting the river, through canals, with the other great waterways of Europe. We shall travel along it, looking at its long history and its exciting new developments.

Right *Remains of much fine pottery have been found in the Danube basin. This figure is 6,000 years old, but some are even older.*

Through Highland Germany

The river Danube begins as a number of little streams in the hilly south-western corner of Germany, called the Black Forest. The two chief streams, the Breg and the Brigach, begin life as trickles of water forming small pools nearly 1,000 m (3,280 ft) above sea level.

The Black Forest area (Schwarzwald in German) is a group of hills to the north of the Alps. Many of the important European rivers, such as the Rhine, begin in the Alps. Where the Danube starts, the Rhine flows only a short distance away, running through its rift valley. But the Rhine is flowing away north, as most great European rivers do. The Danube is unusual, for not only does it not start in the great Alps

Left *A Black Forest stream tumbles towards the Danube*

nearby, but it is the only great European river to flow mainly from west to east. Thus it is able to link together very different areas.

Although the Black Forest is not a high mountain area, the landscape can be impressive. The little streams flow fast down the hillsides, quickly gathering more water as they go, through a rugged, remote landscape thickly covered with pines. Sometimes the country can even seem a little sinister. There are still very few people living here. Only a few decades ago it was said in the towns on the edge of the hills that, in very harsh winters, wolves would sometimes come down from the hills and walk in the streets! With the modern developments of transport and tourism the region is becoming a little less remote, but still the river often flows past nothing but thick clumps of pine forest, huge deserted fields and massive old farmhouses with great thatched roofs and wood-frames made from the pines.

The Breg and the Brigach come together to form the Danube proper at a place called Donaueschingen (Donau is the German word for Danube). We are now passing through a rather broader valley between the Swabian mountains. Sometimes we sail through large gorges, but mostly we pass through rich farming land. On either side of the river are huge fields growing the most varied crops – grains, vegetables, fruit and vines. Near the river itself it is often marshy and there are sometimes peat bogs. The trees, now more often oaks than pines, are well spaced between the fields.

Often, too, we go through or near towns or villages. This rich countryside attracted people to settle very early. For a thousand years there has been a network of rich towns in this area, the homes of traders and craftsmen and, in modern times, of advanced industries.

The first very important town we come to is called Ulm. Here the river has become a wide,

Right *Ulm – an ancient German city by the Danube*

Above *Typical Black Forest scenery*

Left *This library in Ulm is built in the magnificent Baroque style*

powerful stream spanned by a great, arched bridge. Ulm was already a rich and important town in the Middle Ages, six or seven hundred years ago; its minster church has the highest steeple in the world. Today there are still remains of the medieval walls, strong and high enough to repel invaders. Ulm often needed those walls, because this rich and strategically situated countryside has seen the constant passage of armies and invaders. The fierce army of the Huns, led by their notorious king, Attila, crossed the Danube near here in the fifth century A.D. Later they crossed the Rhine and were only finally defeated near Paris by an army of the Romans and Visigoths.

Many of the terrible battles of the Thirty Years' War were fought near here. This was one of the most devastating wars in history, fought in the seventeenth century. In this war a third of the population of Germany were killed. The battle of Blenheim, in 1704, was also fought near here. In this battle the great English general, Marlborough (an ancestor of Sir Winston Churchill) won a famous victory over the French king Louis XIV. A century later another French ruler, Napoleon, had better luck and defeated an Austrian army at Ulm. Even in modern times Ulm has not always had a peaceful existence, for it was heavily bombed in the Second World War. Now huge concrete skyscrapers have replaced many of the ancient merchants' houses.

We come soon to Regensburg. Here the river reaches its most northerly point, turning away

Above *The Austrian General surrenders to Napoleon at the Battle of Ulm in 1805*

from the Franconian mountains to the north and beginning to flow entirely through the Bavarian plateau. Regensburg was a Roman frontier town in A.D. 179. It was from near here that the Romans built a wall, called the Limes, which marked the northern frontier of their empire. It ran from here, cross-country towards the Rhine.

Regensburg has been a great city for many centuries. But it will soon be important in a new way. For many years Regensburg has been the highest point along the river that most large boats could go, although some smaller boats could reach Ulm. This is one reason why Regensburg has been chosen to be at the centre of the great new canal system which is to link the Rhine and Danube. This is to be completed by 1989. The canal will start on the Rhine at Mainz; at Bamberg it will join an old canal, widened and improved, that already goes to Regensburg. When it is completed, boats will be able to travel right across Europe from the Rhine to the Black Sea.

Below *At Passau the Rhine leaves West Germany for Austria*

Above *Two powerful rivers, the Danube and the Inn, at their junction at Passau*

Now the river flows through the flat landscape of the Bavarian plateau, a rather lonely countryside far from the modern centres of development in bustling West Germany. In comparison with the rest of this prosperous country, this area is rather poor. Near the town of Passau the border with Austria is reached. Here, too, the Danube is joined by one of its important tributaries, the Inn. This river drains the Austrian Alpine region called the Tyrol. The Danube has many tributaries, many of them longer and more powerful than any river in Britain, France or Germany. They generally begin in icy Alpine regions and may flood badly in spring. The Inn at Passau, in fact, carries more water than the Danube itself!

So we pass into Austria, one of the most beautiful and interesting stretches of the river, as we travel through a small country that is full of history and interest.

Above *An old picture showing how the Danube becomes more turbulent as it enters Austria*

Into Austria

Immediately we enter Austria the scenery changes. The river valley narrows; on both sides there are hills, sometimes covered with dark forest and sometimes with sheer boulder-strewn cliffs. The river has been falling steeply up to here and it continues to do so – in the Austrian course, at a rate of 1 m (3.3 ft) for every 2 km (1.2 miles). The river is turbulent as well as steep. It is swollen by the waters of the river Inn and deposits so much silt that the river is very shallow in places and flows over rocks in the river bed. Many of these rocks have now been dynamited away, while dams and embankments have been built to ease the passage of river craft.

The first big town we come to is called Linz. This is an ancient town with some attractive old houses, but in recent years it has been developing rapidly and it is now more a busy industrial town than a tourist centre. In recent years,

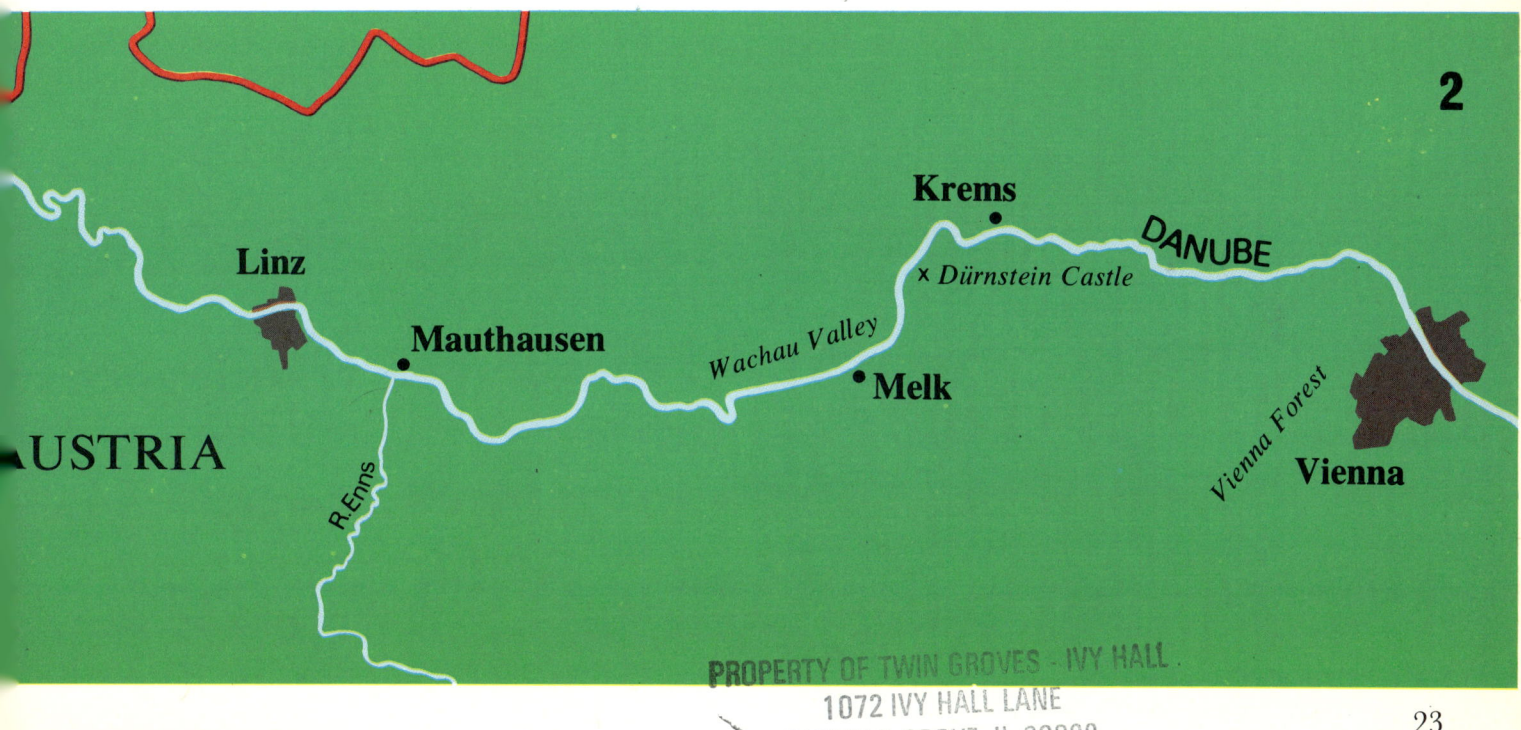

24 **Above** *Here the Danube winds through the steep and lovely valley of the Wachau*

Austria, formerly a rather poor and not heavily populated country, has been developing very fast. In modern Linz, the change is plain to see.

After Linz, however, the landscape loses its forbidding character entirely and we enter a beautiful valley between the Bohemian Forest mountains and the Alps. This valley is called the Wachau. The river twists between the steep hills on which we see vineyards and orchards on the slopes below dark woods. On the slopes, too, are a seemingly endless string of castles, the homes of noble Austrian families for many centuries. Some of these families still live in the castles.

One of these castles, Dürnstein, is especially interesting because it was here that the English king, Richard I, called the Lionheart, was imprisoned by his enemy the Duke of Austria on his way home from Jerusalem after the Third Crusade in 1193–4. Legend has it that he was found in this prison by his faithful minstrel Blondel who sang beneath every castle wall in the area until the prisoner heard his voice! Richard was later released on the payment of a huge ransom, on the proceeds of which the Austrians were able to build a couple of cities.

Soon after we enter the Wachau, the river Enns adds its waters to those of the Danube. A short way up this tributary is the little town of Steyr where the great composer Schubert wrote his famous and beautiful "Trout Quintet". Perhaps Schubert's trout was swimming towards the Danube! The Danube is, in fact, tremendously rich in fish life, with over seventy different

Above *Durnstein Castle on a craggy rock, where Richard the Lionheart was imprisoned*

Above *The Great Abbey of Melk, on a hill above the river*

species. This is because the river is a link between the fish species of western Europe and those that populate the rivers of the Soviet Union. It has its own kind of salmon and two distinct types of pike-perch, as well as the giant catfish which measures up to 4 m (13 ft). It is sad that the growing pollution of the river is decreasing this magnificent abundance of life.

Near the junction with the Enns, on the north side of the river, we come to the sleepy little village of Mauthausen which, through no fault of its own, has acquired a terrible reputation. This was where a concentration camp was built in 1938 by the German Nazi regime, under Hitler, after they had conquered Austria. Hitler and the Nazis believed that all peoples of German origin should be united in one country and the other peoples of Europe should be their slaves. More than 30,000 people were murdered in this camp, mainly Jews and people who would not agree with the Nazis. The site of the old camp is now open to visitors and it serves as a warning to future generations of the evil that can be done by tyrannical governments.

Soon, however, we come to a building that represents very different values and traditions. This is the huge Benedictine abbey of Melk, a truly magnificent building which stands on a cliff above the river. In the Middle Ages many monasteries were built in the area along the river to bring religion and culture to the people. Melk has been destroyed a number of times, but it has always been rebuilt. The present abbey is built in the splendour of the Baroque style which flourished in the seventeenth and eighteenth centuries. For seven hundred years Melk has been a great centre of learning. Its library holds hundreds of precious ancient manuscripts. As we pass, we can see this great building reflected in the water. It is a beautiful sight.

Beyond Krems the Wachau ends, so that flat land takes the place of the hills on the river's northern side. To the south, too, the Alpine ranges are petering towards an end in the wooded hills of the Wienerwald (Vienna Forest in English). There are other great mountains to the east, but this is one of the few places where the Danube breaks through the Alpine system of mountains. It was perhaps inevitable that a great city should grow up at this crossroads of Europe. That city is Vienna, the capital of Austria.

People who see the Danube for the first time at Vienna might well be a little disappointed. The

Above *The Danube is a wide, busy river by the time it reaches Vienna*

river used to flow through the city in various swampy channels during the last century, but it now flows in an artificial canal. The old river can be seen at the outskirts of the city. The Danube is very wide here; it would be a good five minutes walk from one bank to another. The water is starting to get rather dirty, too, for Vienna is a great port and industrial centre. The river here has become famous owing to Johann Strauss's waltz, "The Blue Danube", but, in

Below *The Danube winding through countryside near Vienna*

fact, the water at this point is more brown than blue! Near the river there are factories and warehouses, but there are also attractive parks. Some parts of the old, many-channelled river, now turned into peaceful lakes, can be seen in the large Danube Park (Donau Park), beautifully laid out on the river's northern bank.

For 2,000 years Vienna has been the most important crossroads of Europe. Here, in the lowland gap between the ranges of mountains, the east-west route following the Danube meets the ancient "Amber Road". This was an ancient trade route, linking the Adriatic and Baltic seas. Thus, whoever controlled the city was bound to be powerful. The Romans built a fort here 2,000 years ago. In the ninth century A.D. the great Frankish king, Charlemagne, made Vienna an outpost of his empire which then covered most of western Europe. Ever since then, Vienna has been a frontier, heavily defended against all attacks from the east.

In the sixteenth and seventeenth centuries, the Turks, who had conquered all of south-eastern Europe, often seemed to be threatening Vienna. The greatest siege was in 1683 when a Turkish army, which also included a motley horde of Slavs, Tartars and Magyars, threatened the city. The Turkish sultan sent into the city a gruesome ultimatum. It said, "We shall destroy you and wipe all traces of unbelievers off the face of the earth. With no regard for age, we shall put all through excruciating tortures before we give them death...." The Austrians answered by

Above *Part of the Hofburg Palace, Vienna*

barricading themselves within the city. Eventually the emperor was able to drive the Turks off, but only after he had received support from Poland, Saxony, Franconia and Bavaria.

Today, too, Vienna is a frontier, for about 50 km (30 miles) to the east is the frontier which separates the countries of western Europe from the socialist countries of eastern Europe, almost all of which are under the domination of the Soviet Union.

But, in spite of its position and troubled his-

Below *A banqueting hall in the Hofburg Palace, a home of the Austrian Hapsburg dynasty*

tory, Vienna is a beautiful and cheerful city and its people love life. The city is full of beautiful buildings from the medieval St Stephen's cathedral to the wonderful palaces of the Baroque era. The city enjoyed its greatest days when, for the three centuries before 1918, it was the capital of the Austro-Hungarian Empire which covered the greater part of south-eastern Europe. It was rich and magnificent then; a throng of people of many nationalities filled its streets. It was the home of many famous men, especially great composers – Mozart, Haydn, Beethoven, Schubert, Mahler, the Strauss family, Brahms, Wolf and many more.

Today it still has something of the atmosphere of those great days: you can see the marvellous palaces of the Hapsburgs, the ruling family of the empire; you can walk in the great parks of the city (there are 898 of them in all!) or sit with the Viennese and sip coffee, the great national drink. The Viennese love food and drink; there are countless varieties of coffee served with the most wonderful and creamiest of cakes. Some Viennese, who have given up concern with their waistlines, are known to consume five meals a day!

We leave Vienna with regret, but it is still 2,000 km (1,240 miles) to the sea. We have a little way to go in Austria, but the landscape has changed for ever – we have left the high valleys of the upland course and from now on we shall be passing through the varied landscapes of the plains of south-eastern Europe.

Above *The spendid Belvedere Gardens at Vienna*

The Great Plains

Beyond Vienna the Danube changes its character. So far, it has been flowing in narrow valleys between the Alps or older hill masses. The mountains are continued eastwards from Vienna, and in a few places the river cuts through them in spectacular gorges. But generally, now, the river flows through broad plains – in the 2,000 km (1,240 miles) between Vienna and the sea the Danube falls less than 1 m (3.3 ft) for every 10 km (6 miles). It floods and deposits silt over a very wide area and breaks into many channels. The silt has led to the formation of many islands, often covered with reeds and willow trees. Marshy fields, often empty except for cattle, stretch away from the river. This sort of landscape will be with us all the way to the sea except in the gorge sections, but it is subtly varied as we pass through the different regions. Different peoples have everywhere set their own stamp on the countryside.

We are moving into other national territories now. Up to here the river has been flowing through areas where the people speak German. Fifty km (31 miles) after Vienna we reach the border with Czechoslovakia, but Hungary is very

Left *The Danube on an icy day at Bratislava*

Above *Barge traffic at Bratislava*

close too. In this area there has been a complex intermingling of Teutonic (German), Slavic and Magyar (Hungarian) peoples.

In the endlessly flat area the frontiers have shifted constantly. The last region of Austria we pass through, the Marchfeld (meaning mossy and marshy land on the other shore) has seen wars between Romans and Germanic tribes, the invasions of Huns, Avars and Magyars, medieval pitched battles between the Germanic empire and the kingdoms of Bohemia and Hungary, and, later, Turkish domination.

Bratislava is the first city we come to once we have crossed into Czechoslovakia. It stands where the plain meets the Little Carpathian Mountains, and its history illustrates the complex and troubled past of this region very well. Bratislava is its Czech name, but it is known as Pressburg in German and Pozony in Hungarian. When all Hungary south of the Danube was ruled by the Turks, the city became the Hungarian capital and the kings of Hungary were crowned here between 1536 and 1784. Later on, the city became part of the Austro-Hungarian Empire, ruled over by the German Hapsburg monarchs. Then, in 1918 when this empire broke up, it became part of the newly independent republic of Czechoslovakia. This country made a brief, brave experiment with democratic government, but then fell victim first to Hitler's Nazi empire and then to the Soviet Union, which imposed Communist rule on the people in 1948.

So, as might be expected, Bratislava is a cosmopolitan place, with descendents of people of many nationalities living there. It is an important centre, manufacturing textiles and timber goods. The city is very modern, with many new apartment blocks, although often they are of

Above *Bratislava – a Czechoslovak town with a long history*

rather poor quality. Another vast new waterway system is planned to link the Danube at Bratislava with the river Vistula in Poland, and so to the Baltic Sea.

A short way from Bratislava, the Danube becomes the Czechoslovak-Hungarian border for 240 km (150 miles); then it flows east into Hungary. The river now flows in innumerable loops and bends. The marshy territory in between has often been the subject of disputes between

Czechs and Hungarians. Hundreds of islands are found in the river. One of these, Koz, at the beginning of the Little Hungarian Plain, is 50 km (31 miles) long and 20 km (12 miles) wide, with over a hundred villages. On the Czech side of the stream there are many more islands.

Near the point where the Danube leaves Czechoslovak territory is the historic Hungarian town of Esztergom, for 300 years the home of the kings of Hungary and the traditional headquarters of the Roman Catholic Church in Hungary.

In this country, as in Poland, Communist rule has not succeeded in destroying the power of the Catholic Church over the minds of the people. Esztergom has a magnificent cathedral rich in beautiful works of art. For a town with such an important history, however, it is a rather sleepy place, although it is popular with the many tourists who are increasingly visiting Hungary.

Now the river flows through a gorge section through the Bakony Forest hills, at the southern edge of which the Hungarian capital, Budapest,

Below *The "Danube Bend" area, before the river reaches Budapest*

is found. This region is known as "The Danube Bend". The hills are broken and many pretty little towns and villages lie on their lower slopes. Very often, as in the Austrian Wachau, the hilltops are crowned with castles. Many of these castles were built by kings of the Árpád dynasty of Hungary. The Magyar people burst into the area which is now called Hungary in A.D. 896 under their fierce leader Árpád. His descendants, who ruled until the fourteenth century, built these sturdy castles to repel Tartars and other invaders. The beautiful town of Visegrad in this area began as a place of imprisonment used by the Árpád kings. Later it became a magnificent royal palace until it was destroyed by the Turks in the fifteenth century.

As it leaves the gorge, the river turns suddenly southwards and broadens out into two streams. Between them stretches an island, 50 km (31 miles) long, called Szentendrei. Opposite the island's southern tip we come to the Hungarian capital – Budapest.

Below   *The great city of Budapest, capital of Hungary*

Above *Buda Castle, which has stood guard over Budapest for many centuries*

It was Celtic tribesmen in prehistoric times who first settled here. Later the Romans built a fort here, and in the Middle Ages the Árpád kings built a fortress on the great hill on the right bank of the river. This later became the nucleus of the more ancient part of the city, Buda. Budapest now has nearly two million inhabitants.

Budapest is a beautiful city. Much of its beauty it owes to the great river that flows through it. It is an unforgettable experience to stroll along the embankment in the more modern left-bank part of the city, called Pest, among the gaily-dressed crowds and open-air cafés, and to look across the river to Buda Hill crowned with its ancient fortress. Beyond that you can see the rolling hills, thickly covered with woods, in which the citizens of Budapest love to wander for hours on sunny summer evenings. In the middle of the river you can see many islands. On Margrit Island there are magnificent hotels, beautifully planted gardens and a huge open-air swimming pool with naturally heated water from one of the many warm springs found in or near the city.

We see many Danube boats, too, for Budapest is an important river port; steamships began running between Vienna and Budapest in 1830

Left *A pleasure craft sailing past Budapest*

Above *A Hungarian shepherd in the Great Plains*

and there was once an extensive passenger service between the two cities. This has almost totally stopped, but boats still pass constantly through the city on their way both downstream and upstream. If we get tired of this varied scene, we can go away from the river into the city itself which has many fine avenues and parks mainly laid out in the nineteenth century.

We leave this lively city for a rather more lonely region. South of Budapest, the river enters the Great Hungarian Plain. Here the "flatland" character of the river is at its most striking; hundreds of channels, with as many islands, meander aimlessly across a land full of willows, reeds and brown marshes. Few people can live here because the land is so unstable. The villages that we do see are large, sometimes as large as towns, although the people in them are all farmers. This is partly because there is so little dry land and partly because of the troubled history of the area, so that people have always lived close to each other for defence. The villages are generally built a little distance from the river because of the danger of flooding. The floods have also made bridge building impossible until recent times. We sometimes see a few isolated farms from the river too. They have all been "collectivized" by the Communist government. This means that groups of smaller farms have been joined together to make one large unit, run by all the local farmers together. Many of these farms are now agricultural research centres. Another common sight is fields full of fine horses, of which the Hungarians have been great breeders for centuries.

One interesting town we come to is Mohács. Here, in 1526, was fought one of the greatest battles in European history, in which the Hungarian army was defeated by the Turks. The Turks then took over most of the country for 150 years. To this day, the Hungarians, when faced with some great disaster, will often say, "More men were lost at Mohács" to cheer themselves up!

As the river enters Yugoslavia the landscape does not change dramatically, but we enter an area that has a very distinctive history and culture. This we must now examine.

Above *Fields of fine horses are a common sight in Hungary*

Above *The bustling, modern industrial city of Novi Sad in Yugoslavia*

To the Iron Gates

The region of Yugoslavia that we now enter is called the Voivodina (meaning territory ruled by a count). The land is endlessly flat, like the Great Hungarian Plain, but it is more fertile. Then the river flows through the Fruška Gora mountains where it turns eastward towards the regional capital of Novi Sad. This is a bustling place where many huge new factories mark Yugoslavia's rapid progress from an agricultural country to an industrial power.

The Voivodina is a fascinating region because, even in south-eastern Europe which is famed for its complex mixing of peoples, it has an amazing mixture of nationalities. Yugoslavs are the main nationality, but many of them have migrated from other regions of Yugoslavia, so even they are a great mixture. There are also many Hungarians and Romanians and even some descendants of the Turks live here. Schools, newspapers, radio, television, all use a great variety of

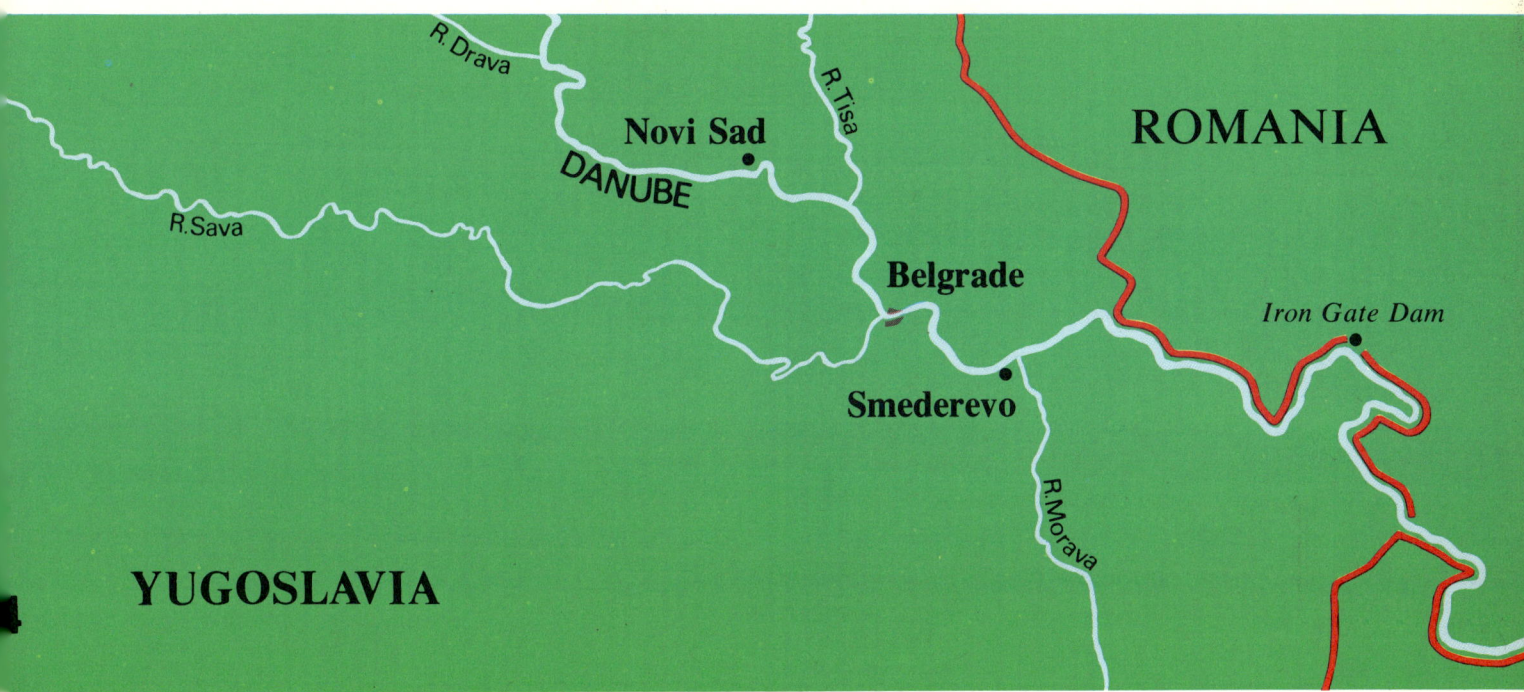

43

Above *Novi Sad, capital of the Voivodina area*

languages — five are used on the radio, for instance. The Voivodina has a considerable measure of self-government because the Yugoslav government has found that the only way to cope with the amazing mixture of peoples in the country (there are six major groupings among the Yugoslavs alone) is to allow the various localities a large say in running their own affairs. This is one of the many unusual features of Yugoslav Communism, which has been very independent since the country broke free from the Soviet Union in 1948.

One of the reasons why so many people have settled in the Voivodina is that, unlike the marshy plain of Hungary, it is excellent farming land. As it flows through the area, the Danube passes hundreds of quiet little towns and villages. Many of them have ancient water mills working in the streams and churches with miniature domes like mosques (a sign of Turkish influence) rather than the spires you see in western Europe. Great rafts of logs can often be seen in this region floating down the river — for centuries the Danube has had a flourishing timber trade

Above *The lush green countryside of the Voivodina*

transported in this way. A common sight, too, are flocks of wild geese flying among the numerous silver birch trees. It is not perhaps a very exciting landscape, but it is an attractive one.

Many important tributaries join the Danube in Yugoslavia, swelling its waters enormously. In the Voivodina, the Danube is joined by the rivers Drava and Tisa, both of which are powerful enough to cause a great bend in the river where the joining takes place. The Tisa is longer even than the Rhine, the greatest river of western Europe. All these rivers can do massive damage in flooding; in bad years the flow of the Tisa can be fifty times as great as when it is at its lowest point! Large programmes of dams and embankments are being developed by the Yugoslavs to guard against these dangers.

The capital of Yugoslavia – Belgrade – is found at the point where the Danube is joined by its most important tributary, the Sava. Two thousand five hundred years ago a Celtic fort was built on the Kalemegdan, the hill overlooking the point where the two great rivers join. Later, both Romans and Turks built important

Left *Belgrade is the third great capital city found along the Danube. The others are Vienna and Budapest*

fortifications here at this strategic point. Now it serves a more peaceful purpose as a park area where the citizens of Belgrade are able to enjoy their leisure hours.

Throughout its long history Belgrade has been repeatedly destroyed. Twice in the Second World War it was almost bombed out of existence. This explains why it looks so very modern today.

The reason for all these attacks is that, as a great route centre, its position has immense importance. The fact that it lies at the junction of so many routes also explains why it has been able to hold its position as the capital of Yugoslavia. In the nineteenth century Belgrade was the capital of Serbia, which was one of the few parts of the Balkans free from either Turkish or Austro-Hungarian rule. Later, in 1918, when both these empires collapsed, areas where mainly southern Slavic peoples (Yugoslavs) lived were joined to Serbia in the new kingdom of Yugoslavia. After the Second World War, this became Communist. Belgrade, which has river valley connections with four of Yugoslavia's six present-day republics, is in an ideal position to hold together this varied and sometimes troubled country.

Below *The Kalemegdan Hill in Belgrade, a fortress for centuries but now a pleasant park*

Above *Smederevo, the ancient fortress used by the Turks to subdue Yugoslavia*

Another Yugoslav republic, Macedonia, can be reached by sailing up the Morava, which flows into the Danube near Smederevo, east of Belgrade. Here there is an ancient Turkish fortress which helped the Turks to rule after they conquered Serbia in the sixteenth century. It guarded a very important route, for people going to south-eastern Europe (and, beyond that, to Asia) have, for many centuries, followed the river route via the Sava, Danube and Morava. The great German emperor, Frederick Barbarossa, travelled this way when he went on the Third Crusade in the early 1190s, only to drown in a ditch as he was crossing present-day Turkey. If you went on an overland trip today to India or Pakistan you would, no doubt, follow the same route as he did, although hopefully with more fortunate results!

About 40 km (25 miles) to the east of Smederevo, we approach one of the most spectacular regions of our journey – the series of huge gorges called the Iron Gates found at the border area between Yugoslavia and Romania. There are eight separate gorges; the name "Iron Gates" is sometimes applied to all of them, although, strictly speaking, it applies only to the lowest and most dangerous of the gorges.

As we approach them, perhaps on a long-distance passenger boat or on the lonely road winding over the Serbian hills, their beauty and

Right *The River Sava joins the Danube at Belgrade*

Left *The Danube flowing between steep crags in the Iron Gorge region*

majesty is very striking. The river enters them very narrowly between the Carpathian and Serbian mountains. It seems to be flowing right into the very heart of the mountains. Near this impressive entrance, a great jagged stone, called the Babakaj, rises 12 m (40 ft) sheer out of the river.

In the rocks, as we sail through, we can see great caverns from which swarms of flies sometimes emerge to make life miserable for cattle in the surrounding plains. The entrance to the gorge is guarded by castles; for instance, we pass the ruins of the castle of Golubac which was the stronghold of a medieval Serbian dynasty against the Turks. All in all, this is an impressive, even frightening, region.

As we travel into the gorges, sheer mountains begin to rise up on either side, sometimes nearly 1,500 m (5,000 ft) high. The river twists dangerously between the mountains and the life of the sailor is made difficult by rocks, shoals, cataracts and bends. The current can become incredibly powerful and, in places, the depth may be up to 70 m (230 ft).

As you can imagine, navigation in this area has always caused tremendous problems. Even in comparatively recent times top speed for boats was barely 2 km (1 mile) an hour. Getting through the whole region could take more than three days, although the entire distance is only 95 km (60 miles). The most dangerous point was at the Iron Gates proper, a great, eddying froth of rapids over which the river lashed in what seemed like a wild fury. At this point the river became shallower and the banks became closer together; the river narrowed at one point to only 40 m (129 ft)!

The Iron Gates region has been one of the greatest barriers to navigation and human passage in the whole of Europe, but man has been very inventive in solving its problems. Almost

Right *It is impressive, perhaps even frightening, to enter the Iron Gorge by boat*

two thousand years ago, the Romans actually managed to construct a bridge over one of the narrowest and most difficult sections. This was a very impressive achievement because they had few tools, almost no machinery and had to do most of the work with their bare hands. The achievement seems even greater when we reflect that, in all the years between then and 1953, only one bridge had been constructed on the Danube in the whole area between Novi Sad and the sea. Since then a number of huge bridges have been built on the lower Danube.

The Roman bridge was ordered to be constructed by the Emperor Trajan in the early second century A.D. in order to conquer the province of Dacia – what we now call Romania. A beautiful coin, a bronze sestertius, was struck to commemorate the event. Until recently a tablet on a rock at the Iron Gates recorded that this was the place where the bridge had stood for 200 years.

But not any more, because the latest works on the river have been so ambitious as to change some of the landscape completely. About ten years ago, Romanians and Yugoslavs jointly built a gigantic dam across the eastern end of the Iron Gates. This formed a huge and peaceful lake 135 km (84 miles) long. Passenger and cargo boats now have no trouble at all navigating this section. It has become so peaceful that it is even possible to go yachting! The scheme serves many purposes – there is a new bridge and connecting roads, irrigation water and massive generation of hydro-electricity from the new dam. It is a magnificent scheme, but a pity that much beautiful and interesting landscape has been destroyed. For instance, the island of Ada Kaleh has gone for ever. This was an interesting island because, even though it was in Romanian territory, it had belonged to Turkey until 1918 and was still inhabited almost entirely by Turks, who had won many privileges from the Romanian government.

When the dam was being built in 1967, a remarkable discovery was made. At a place called Lepenski Vir, remains of an ancient

Above *The ancient Roman coin showing Trajan's bridge over the Danube*

Above *Black-tailed godwits, wading birds which breed along the Danube*

Danubian settlement were discovered. The remains, which included much beautiful carving, dated back 7,500 years and bore witness to a culture of fairly advanced farming villages which must have existed at that time. More recently, remains of farming settlements have been found lower down the Danube valley, all over Romania and Bulgaria, and in northern Greece. These remains are thought to be over 1,000 years older.

Scholars had thought that agriculture had begun in the Near East and had spread from there around the world. These finds may mean that agriculture developed in Europe at the same time as in the Near East, or even earlier.

So we leave the Iron Gates. The river has still a long way to go to the sea, but from now on our journey will lie entirely through flat plains until we reach the river's most impressive delta.

Towards the Delta

Now we are going through plains again to complete the last section of our journey. Wide and sluggish, the river meanders over a vast area, only occasionally coming together into a single channel. Immediately below the Iron Gates the river is only a little above sea level but it still has nearly 900 km (560 miles) to go before reaching the sea. It will hardly fall any more in the whole remainder of its course.

At first the river forms the border between Romania and Bulgaria. On the Romanian, northern side we can see a vast plain, almost entirely composed of river silt, which extends to the foothills of the Carpathians. Varied crops are grown on this plain – grains, fruit, grapes, vegetables, fodder – but most noticeable, perhaps, are the huge fields of yellow sunflowers that may

Left *A backwater of the Danube delta*

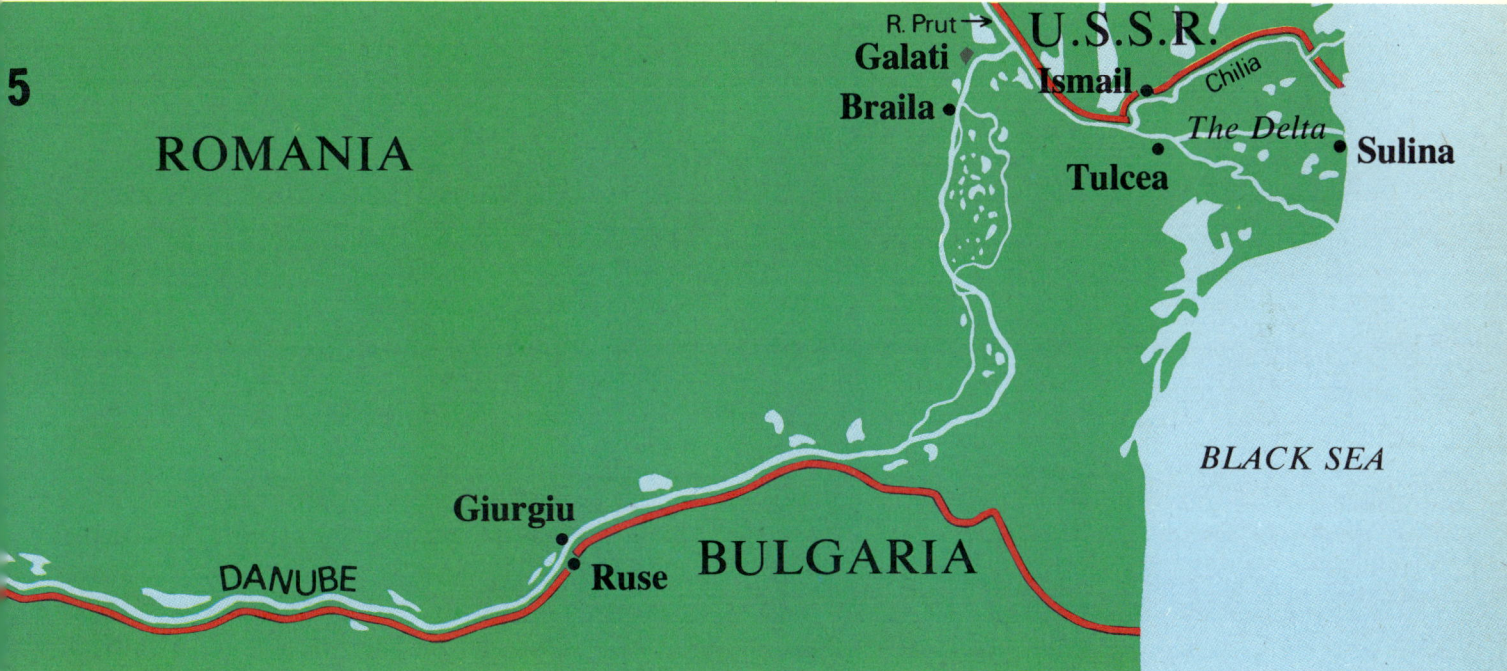

Above *A peasant way of life still survives in parts of Romania*

extend for miles. Near the river there are often lakes and swamps and sometimes divided channels. On the Bulgarian side the land is higher and forms a level, rather featureless plateau with few rivers or towns.

Many of the towns we come to are river ports. One of the most important of these, on the Romanian bank, is Giurgiu. This is where most Danube passenger boats come to their eastern terminus and also where much of the Romanian oil is shipped for transport upstream. It is a typical dock town, with a rather seedy, decaying atmosphere. In the air is always the strong, sour smell of petrol and other cargoes. Hundreds of dockworkers seem to be unloading and loading goods on the quaysides all day. Opposite, on the Bulgarian bank, and linked to Giurgiu by a huge new bridge, is the similar Bulgarian port of

Ruse. This town is famous for a type of whisky made from dried plum skins!

Some way after this the river turns north into completely Romanian territory (the province of the Dobrogea) and we notice an end to the long lines of soldiers' sentry boxes that have marked the frontier. After the large ports of Brăila and Galati we turn east towards the delta. The river is joined by its last great tributary, the Prut, which has previously formed a stretch of the border between Romania and the Soviet Union. Three main channels now carry the river to the

Below *The Danube delta is becoming busier than it was and large ships can now be seen there*

Left *Pelicans and their young – a common sight in the delta, but nowhere else in Europe*

sea, although numerous sub-channels also develop. The most important branch is the northern Chilia arm which forms a border between Romania and the Soviet Union. A small part of the delta is in the U.S.S.R.

The delta is an extraordinary region covering an area of 2,600 sq km (1,000 sq miles). It was only formed during the past 6,500 years, which is very young in geological terms, and the relationship between land and sea in the area is still uncertain and fluctuating. It is mostly water or swampland, but much so-called "land" consists merely of floating reed-islands held together by the reeds' roots which move constantly and cause the water channels to shift with them. Many waters are mere stagnant trickles, while elsewhere there are large lakes. Areas of brown marsh may stretch for long distances. In the air there is an all-pervading smell of mud, reeds and animal dung. This area could perhaps be best looked at by moonlight when it might seem more like some strange, swampy planet than like anywhere on earth! However, a substantial industry has recently been developed, cutting large quantities of reeds and turning them into paper.

The variety of animal life in the area is amazing. It is the only place in Europe where pelicans breed in large numbers. Wolves, polecats, martens, wildcats and other rare species live here. Rare and unusual plants, including one that actually eats insects, are also found. Several nature reserves have been established and, because the region is so remote, there is good

Above *A typical reedy scene in the delta*

Above *A fisherman resting in his reed hut*

hope that this profusion of life, never found in western Europe where there are so many towns and people, will be preserved. In order to ensure this, robbing birds' nests has been made illegal in the area!

Few people can live in such a difficult place. Almost all the inhabitants have come to live here fairly recently. Some, the Lipovani, left Russia to escape religious persecution two hundred years ago; others came from the Ukraine at the end of the last century. Almost all make a precarious living by fishing from little boats roughly the size of Canadian canoes.

In this strange region it is sometimes difficult to tell exactly where the river merges into the Black Sea, the resting place into which the Danube water finally flows. How different is this ending from the river's beginning as two bubbling little streams high up in the Black Forest. But the keynote of the Danube is variety. Journeying along it you can learn what an immensely rich, fascinating and diverse place the continent of Europe can be.

Above *The traditional way of life of the Danube delta, still one of the most remote and wild areas in Europe*

Facts and Figures

Length: 2,850 km (1,770 miles)
Drainage basin: 816,000 sq km (315,000 sq miles)
Discharge: 7,190 cu m (254,000 cu ft) per second
Number of tributaries: about 300
Width at Passau: 211 m (230 yards)
           at Belgrade: 1,560 m (1,706 yards)

Time chart

c. 700 B.C.   Ancient Greeks sailed and traded down the lower Danube.

c. A.D.100–300   Ancient Romans established control over the Danube basin.

c. A.D.300–1000   An age of invasions in central and eastern Europe, before the establishment of settled kingdoms. One important group of people to invade were the Magyars who entered what is now Hungary in A.D.896.

c. 1400–1700   Age of the Turkish onslaught on eastern Europe. Much of the lower Danube basin passed under Turkish rule.

c. 1650–1918   Much of the Danube basin under the rule of the Austro-Hungarian Empire, ruled by the Hapsburg monarchs.

1856   First international commission set up to regulate Danube navigation.

1918   Break-up of the Austro-Hungarian and Turkish empires and setting up of many modern eastern European nations.

1939–1945   The Second World War; much destruction along the Danube banks.

1945–1948   Communist rule imposed by the Soviet Union on many eastern European nations.

1989   Date by which the new system of canals linking the Rhine and Danube will be in operation.

Glossary

Amber Road Ancient European track-route along which various goods, including amber, were carried. It ran from the Adriatic Sea in the south to the Baltic Sea in the north.
Baroque Ornate artistic style, developed during the sixteenth and seventeenth centuries.
Basin The area drained by a river and its *tributaries*.
Benedictine Order of Roman Catholic monks and nuns, founded by St. Benedict.
Celtic peoples Population group once spread widely over Europe and now found mainly in areas such as Ireland, Scotland, Wales and Brittany.
Collective farming Farming organized by a community and not by individual farmers each with his own separate farm.
Crusade Expedition of Christians to win back the Holy Land for Christianity.
Dam Large barrier across a river, built to hold back and store water.
Defile A *gorge*; originally a long pass or way through which troops could march only in single file because it was so narrow.
Delta Triangular-shaped area at the mouth of a river where *silt* is deposited and the river divides into channels.
Embankment Artificial or natural barrier along a river bank, giving protection to low-lying land from river flooding.
Gorge Very narrow and steep-sided part of a river valley.
Hydro-electricity Electricity produced by means of machinery driven by water-power.
Irrigation Spreading water from a river onto fields, using canals etc.
Magyars Population group who were the ancestors of present-day Hungarians; also used to describe one of the largest groups of people in Hungary today.
Meander Bend in a river; very winding course.
Plain Wide, low-lying land.
Plateau High, flat land.
Rift valley Valley made when an area of land is let down between two parallel lines, or faults, in rocks.
Sestertius Ancient Roman coin.
Silt Fine particles of earth, coarser than clay but finer than sand, carried down by a river.
Slavs Eastern European population group speaking one of the Slavic languages.
Teutonic peoples People of the German population group, or speaking a Germanic language.
Tributary River that flows into another, generally larger, one.
Visigoths Ancient warlike people who from the fifth century conquered much of France and Spain.

Further Reading

Edwards, Lovett F. *Danube Stream* (Frederick Muller, 1940).

Lehmann, John *Down River: A Danubian Study* (The Cresset Press, 1939).

Lessner, E. C. *The Danube: a history of the great river and the people touched by its flow* (Greenwood, USA. Distributed in the UK by Westport Publications, 1973).

Popescu, J. *The Danube* (Oxford University Press, 1975).

ACKNOWLEDGEMENTS

Ardea – London page 41 (John Mason); Austrian National Tourist Board page 24; Barnaby's Picture Library pages 20, 21, 28, 32, 36; Camera Press *frontispiece*, pages 16, 29, 31, 40, 60, 61; Czechoslovak Tourist Office (Cedok) pages 34, 35; Radio Times Hulton Picture Library pages 19, 22, 25; Sonia Halliday and Laura Lushington pages 12, 30; Robert Harding pages 37, 44, 45, 48, 51; Eric Hosking page 52; Picturepoint pages 46, 47, 49; Romanian National Tourist Office pages 54, 58; Ronald Sheridan pages 8–9, 11, 13; B. A. Seaby Ltd. page 52; Spectrum Colour Library pages 14, 26, 27, 38, 39, 50, 56, 57, 59; Verkehrsburo der Stadt Ulm pages 17, 18; Yugoslavian Tourist Office page 42. Artwork by Alan Gunston, Michael Paysden and Celia Ware.

Index

ps 13, 15, 21, 27, 29, 30, 33
ber Road 29
ncient settlements 12, 39, 45, 52, 53
nimal life 40, 43, 51, 59, 60
rpád and Árpád Kings 37, 39
ttila the Hun 19, 34
ustria 9, 12, 21, 23, 24, 26, 27, 28, 29, 30, 33, 34
ustro-Hungarian Empire 29, 30, 34, 47

bakaj 31
aroque Style 27, 30
elgrade 12, 45, 47
lack Forest 15, 16, 60
lack Sea 20, 60
enheim 19
ondel 24
áila 57
atislava 34, 35
eg River 15, 16
igach River 15, 16
dapest 12, 36, 37, 39, 40
lgaria 9, 12, 55, 56, 57

rpathians 13, 34, 51, 55
arlemagne, Emperor of France 29
ommunism in eastern Europe 12, 29, 34, 40, 44, 47

nube River
 bridges 40, 52, 56
 canals 13, 20, 28
 dams and embankments 23, 45, 52
 delta 57, 59, 60
 drainage basin 9
 floods 10, 33, 40, 45
 formation 13
 islands 10, 33, 36, 39, 40, 52, 59
 length 9
 navigation difficulties 10, 20, 23, 48, 51, 52
 source 15, 16
 traffic on 9, 10, 12, 13, 28, 39, 40, 44, 56
Donaueschingen 16
Drava River 45
Dürnstein 24

Esztergom 36

Farming 16, 40, 43, 53, 55, 56
Fish life and fishing 24, 26, 60
Frederick Barbarossa, Emperor of Germany 48

Galati 57
Giurgiu 56
Golubac 51
Great Hungarian Plain 40
Greeks, ancient 12
Gypsies 13

Hapsburgs 30, 34
Hungary 9, 12, 13, 30, 34, 35, 36, 40, 44

Industry 16, 28, 34, 43, 59
Inn River 21, 23
Iron Gates gorges 48, 51, 52, 53

Kalemegdan 45, 47
Koz Island 36

Lepenski Vir 52, 53
Linz 23, 24
Louis XIV, King of France 19

Marchfeld 34
Mauthausen 26, 27
Melk 27
Mohács 40

Morava River 43

Napoleon, Emperor of France 19
Nazis 26, 27, 34
Novi Sad 43, 52

Passau 21
Prut River 57

Regensburg 19, 20
Rhine River 9, 15, 20
Richard I, the Lionheart, King of England 24
Romania 9, 12, 48, 52, 55, 56, 57, 59, 60
Romans, ancient 12, 19, 20, 34, 52
Ruse 36, 57

Sava River 45, 48
Second World War 19, 47
Serbia 47, 51
Smederevo 48
Soviet Union 9, 12, 26, 29, 34, 44, 57, 59, 60
Strauss family 28, 29, 30

Third Crusade 24, 48
Thirty Years' War 19
Tisa River 45
Turks and Turkish Empire 12, 29, 34, 37, 40, 44, 47, 48, 51, 52

Ulm 16, 19

Vienna 10, 12, 27, 28, 29, 30
Visegrad 37
Voivodina 43, 44
Volga River 9

Wachau 24, 26, 27
West Germany 9, 15, 16, 19, 20, 21

Yugoslavia 9, 12, 40, 43, 44, 45, 47, 48, 51, 52, 53

WOODLAWN MIDDLE SCHOOL
6362 RFD Gilmer RD.
Long Grove, IL 60047
(847) 949-8012